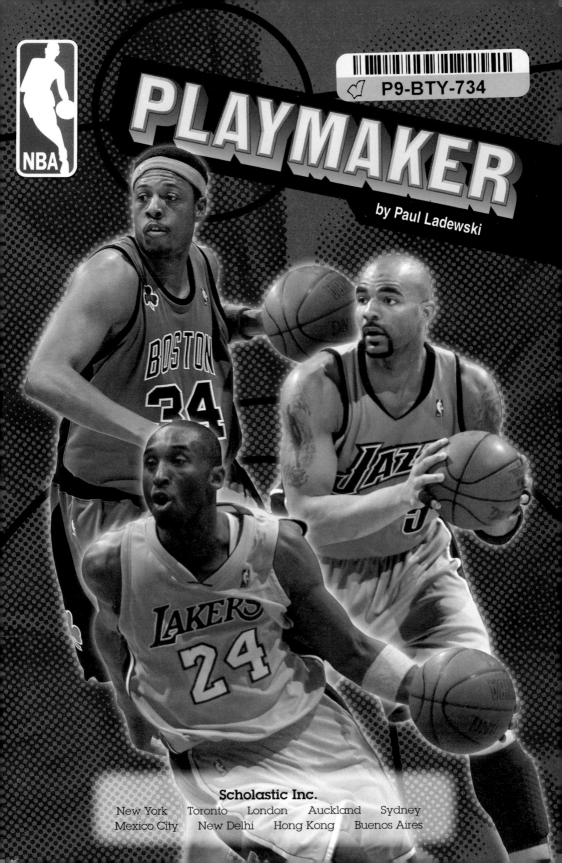

PLAYMAKER

by Paul Ladewski

P9-BTY-734

Scholastic Inc.

New York   Toronto   London   Auckland   Sydney
Mexico City   New Delhi   Hong Kong   Buenos Aires

ISBN-13: 978-0-545-00666-8
ISBN-10: 0-545-00666-X

12 11 10 9 8 7 6 5 4 3 2 1   8 9 10 11 12/ 0

Printed in the U.S.A.
First printing, January 2008

PRACTICE MAKES PERFECT!

So you want to play with the best basketball team on the block, huh? And you want to be the best player on the squad? Here are three words of advice for you — practice, practice, practice.

Ask any NBA head coach and they'll tell you that a player is only as good as their workouts. The ones who pay attention and run the plays correctly in practice are usually the most prepared and confident to play the actual games.

In this book, you will find descriptions of the five positions as well as ex-

planations and diagrams of six offensive and three defensive plays that will help you and your team improve and grow together. For years, these plays have been some of the most popular and successful in the game. As you'll see on the next pages, basketball was, is, and always will be a team game. And the team that plays together has more fun together. Try making plays of your own on the foldout play board at the back of these books, or on the court. And remember, in basketball or anything else, practice makes perfect!

CHEAT SHEET – POSITION DESCRIPTIONS

The five positions in basketball are point guard, off guard, small forward, power forward, and center. They are often described by the numbers (not their uniform numbers though) 1, 2, 3, 4, and 5. In other words, point guard is 1, off guard is 2, and so on.

Here are the descriptions for each position:

1 Point guard: The main responsibility of the 1 is to start the offense at the "point" of attack. He handles the ball more than anyone on the court and tries to get it to the hands of the teammate who has the best chance to score. Jason Kidd, Steve Nash, Chris Paul, and Deron Williams are some of the best NBA players at this position.

2 Off guard: Also called the shooting guard, he sets up without or "off" the ball, opposite the point guard. The 2 should be athletic, able to handle the ball, shoot it from the outside, and run the fast break. Gilbert Arenas, Kobe Bryant, Vince Carter, Allen Iverson, Tracy McGrady, and Dwyane Wade are on the list of top off guards.

3 Small forward: This person is the "smaller" of the two forwards and plays further away from the basket. As a result, the 3 has to be versatile enough to dribble, pass, rebound, and shoot. Carmelo Anthony, Caron Butler, LeBron James, and Shawn Marion are among the best at this position.

4 Power forward: This player has the physical "power" and strength to plant himself close to the basket. Also known as the strong forward, the 4 should be mobile enough to move away from it when necessary. Nobody does this better than Chris Bosh, Elton Brand, Kevin Garnett, Dwight Howard, and Dirk Nowitzki at this position.

5 Center: The 5 is a position of size and physical strength. The main duty of the man in the middle is to patrol the area close to the basket at both ends of the court. He usually is the best rebounder and shot-blocker on the team. Yao Ming and the O'Neals — Jermaine and Shaquille — are tops at this position.

Check out these basketball terms and definitions, straight from NBA.com!

Air ball: A shot that misses the backboard and rim of the basket.

Alley-oop: A pass in which the receiving player catches the ball in the air and shoots the ball without touching the ground.

Assist: A player earns an assist when his pass leads directly to a basket by a teammate.

Backdoor: When a player cuts behind his defender to the basket.

Baseline: The blue-lined mark surrounding the perimeter of the court where all the game action takes place.

Blocked shot: Stopping a shot attempt from reaching the basket before the ball reaches its highest point. Often referred to as a "rejection."

Bounce pass: Passing the ball from one player to another by bouncing it on the floor.

Cylinder: The imaginary "cylindrical" space directly above the rim of the basket. Under NBA rules, the ball cannot be touched when it is in the cylinder.

Double-Double: The feat of collecting ten or more of two statistical categories in one game.

Draft: The selection process to determine on which NBA teams the top newcomers will play.

Dunk: Making a basket by stuffing the ball down through the rim and into the net.

Fast break: A play that occurs when the offensive team quickly gets the ball ahead of the defensive team.

Field Goal: A shooting attempt, missed or successful, by an offensive player during the course of a game.

Free throw: When a foul is committed, the player fouled usually gets to shoot from the free-throw line (which is 15 feet from the basket) without being defended.

Goaltending: A defensive player illegally blocking an opponent's shot attempt when the ball is within the parameters of the rim's cyclinder.

Halftime: The intermission between the first and second halftime — which usually lasts 15 minutes.

Illegal defense: Two defensive players guarding an offensive opponent without possession of the ball.

Jump shot: An offensive attempt by any of the five players on the court.

Lane: The painted area from the end line under the basket to the free-throw line.

Layup: An offensive attempt other than a jump shot whereby a player lays the ball off the backboard, and into the basket.

Paint: See "lane" above.

Pass: The passing of the ball, either using a chest or bounce pass, to turn over possession of the ball to a teammate.

Quadruple-double: The rare feat of collecting ten or more of four statistical categories during one game.

Personal Foul: A violation committed by one player against another player. Following his sixth personal foul, the player is disqualified for the rest of the game.

Rebound: Controlling the ball following a missed shot.

Reserve: A player sitting on the bench other than the five currently competing in the game.

Rookie: A player with no prior NBA experience, who usually is acquired in the NBA Draft.

Screen: The act of delaying or preventing an opponent from reaching a position without causing undue contact.

Shot clock: The shot clock is used to time possessions. The offensive team has 24 seconds to make a scoring attempt.

Shooting guard: Known primarily for their scoring and ballhandling, the shooting guard is usually one of the team's top offensive weapons.

Sixth man: Refers to the team's first player off the bench, after the starting five.

Steal: Taking the ball away from an opponent or intercepting a pass.

Swing-man: A player who can "swing" back and forth and play two positions.

Technical foul: A technical foul is assessed by violations such as illegal defense, as well as player and coach misconduct.

Three-point shot: A shot attempted by a player from beyond an arc distanced at 23 feet, 9 inches.

Three-second violation: When an offensive player is in the lane more than three seconds.

Time-out: A requested break in action by a team either with the possession of the ball, or when the ball is dead.

Trillion: A stat line in which a player fails to collect either a shot, point, rebound, assist, or foul, thus resulting in a stat line of all zeros.

Triple-double: The feat of collecting ten or more of three statistical categories in one game.

Turnover: A miscue that results in a change of possession of the ball.

Weak side: The portion of the defensive team on the court furthest away from the offensive player with possession of the ball.

KEY

Use this key to help you understand all the symbols in the play diagrams. Then you can use the symbols to make your own plays on the court on the back cover.

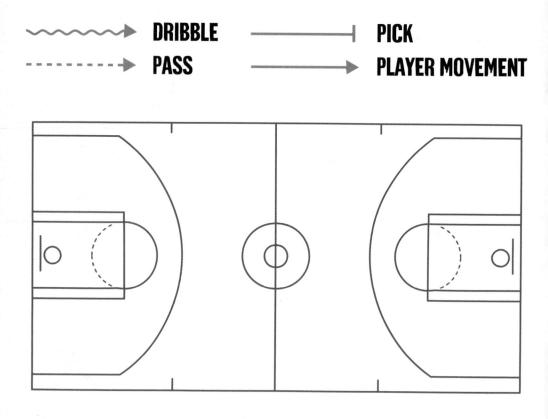

〜〜〜➤ **DRIBBLE**   ————⊣ **PICK**

--------➤ **PASS**   —————➤ **PLAYER MOVEMENT**

1 **POINT GUARD**

2 **SHOOTING GUARD**   ☐ **DEFENSE**

3 **SMALL FORWARD**

4 **POWER FORWARD**   ◯ **OFFENSE**

5 **CENTER**

THE PLAYS

Double-Team
Full-Court Press
Half-Court Trap
Back Door
Fast Break

Give and Go
Lob Pass
Post Up
Screen and Roll

DOUBLE-TEAM

Key positions:
Point guard, off guard, center.

The goal:
To help a defender who is matched against a stronger, taller and/or more talented player close to the basket. (Hey, think it's easy for one person to guard against Tim Duncan or Shaquille O'Neal by himself?) It also can work effectively against a big player who is slow to react and is not a strong passer.

How the Double-Team works:
After the offensive player receives a pass in or near the three-second lane in front of the basket (also known as "the paint" because of its color), one of the guards leaves his assignment to harass the big man from behind, if possible. This is done immediately, either when the ball is passed, the player catches the ball, or he makes a move for it. (It is best for the defense to change the pattern regularly so the man in the middle will not know what to expect.) Because the double-team leaves one player open, the other three defenders have to be prepared to rotate quickly in the event of another pass.

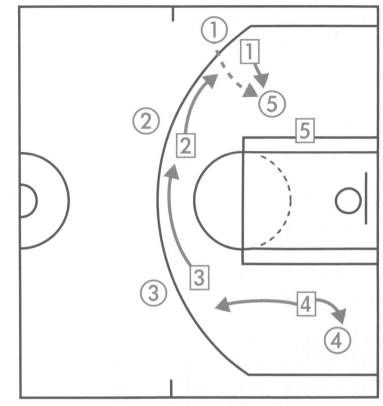

"Because teams would rather give up an outside shot rather than one close to the basket, this strategy has become common at the pro level in recent years."

FULL-COURT PRESS

Key positions:
Point guard, off guard, small forward.

The goal:
To pressure opponents to give up the ball (also known as "turnovers") and score easy baskets as a result. It is often used when a team is be-hind and needs to score points in a hurry, or to take advantage of an opponent who is unsure with the ball.

How the Full-court Press works:
It can be done in any number of ways, but all of them require energy and aggressiveness. Defenders cover their assigned players as closely as the rules allow to either force a mistake if they have the ball or keep it out of their hands if they don't. (Think Dobermans!) Or, two or even three defenders blanket the ball handler in an attempt to force an inaccurate pass or other error. All the while, the defense should do whatever possible to keep the opponent guards out of the play and force their bigger teammates to handle the ball.

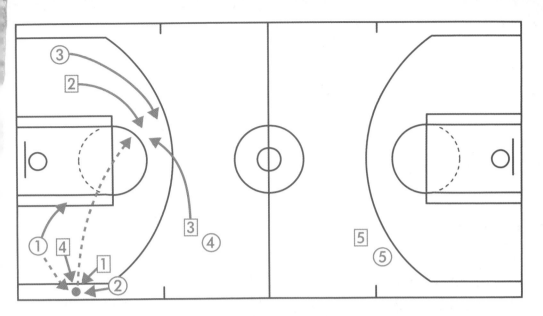

"This is one of the best ways to scramble the game and take the other team out of its rhythm, but it requires players in great physical condition to make it work effectively."

HALF-COURT TRAP

Key positions:
Point guard, off guard.

The goal:
To double-team the ball handler near mid-court and force him to make a mistake of some kind. In that case, the result can be an easy basket.

How the Half-Court Trap works:
After the ball handler crosses the mid-court line, the two closest defenders pursue him aggressively and try to "trap" the ball as a way to either take it away or force a hurried pass. The other three defenders stay on their assigned players, but they must be prepared to cover the unguarded player immediately if a pass is made to him. If a successful pass is made, then the two closest defenders collapse on him and so forth. All the while, the open player should be the one farthest away from the ball. That way it would take a longer, more difficult pass for him to get it.

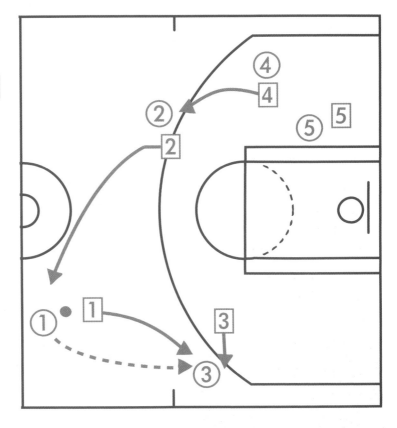

An NBA scout says: "This can be a very effective defense for teams that have quick, experienced players. What makes it work is the ability to rotate smartly and immediately, which takes lots of practice."

NJNETS.COM

BACK DOOR

Key positions:

Off guard, small forward, center.

The goal:

This play is intended to take advantage of defenders that are aggressive and/or slow on their feet. It can be very effective with a big man who passes the ball accurately from several feet away from the basket (a system known as the "high-post offense"), and active teammates such as Manu Ginobili and Richard Hamilton, who move well without the ball around them.

How the Back Door works:

Late for dinner? Then you try to sneak in the back door, right? This play is no different. The ball handler sets up on the wing, then passes to a teammate in or near the center of the court. Either the ball handler or another teammate fakes a move to the outside, then cuts sharply to the basket for a return pass and a possible layup. Or if the defender is focused only on him, a wing player can pretend to catch a pass, then make a surprise cut to the bucket for a real pass and a close-in shot.

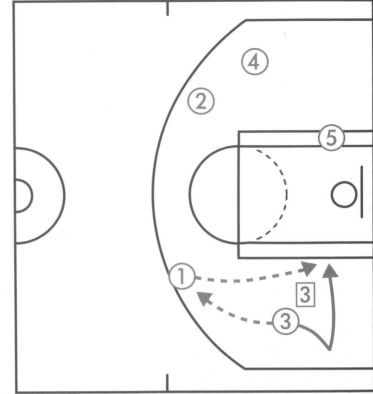

"Coaches call this play to keep defenses honest. What that means is, because of the possibility that the player he is assigned to can sneak behind him for an easy basket, the defender has to back off and give him some room."

FAST BREAK

Key positions:

Point guard, off guard, small forward.

The goal:

To push the ball up the court at a rapid pace, beat the defense before it can set up, and score easy baskets. Jason Kidd and Steve Nash do it better than anyone.

How the Fast Break works:

Actually, it almost always begins at the defensive end, because a team cannot run if it doesn't have the ball. When the team gains possession of the ball, it should be put in the hands of the best ball handler immediately. The other guard fills the lane at one side of the court, the fastest forward fills the lane at the other side, and the ball handler advances the ball in the middle of the court as swiftly as possible. At a point fairly close to the basket, usually near the free-throw line, the ball handler chooses any one of several options. Depending on how the defender(s) react, he can either 1) pass to a player on the left wing; 2) pass to a player on the right wing; 3) pull up for an open shot; or 4) drive to the basket for a better one.

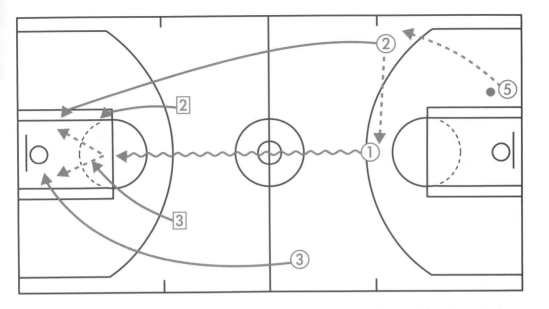

An NBA scout says:

"For teams that have an excellent passer/ball handler and several athletic, well-conditioned players around him, this is the best way to put up points in a hurry and tire out opponents at the same time."

GIVE-AND-GO

Key players:

Point guard, small forward.

The goal:

To surprise a defender who lacks focus or experience or both. It also can be used to help a player shake loose from a defender who is stuck

to him like Velcro. Mike Bibby is a master at the "back cut," as it is also called around the league.

How the Give-and-Go works:

The ball handler gives up the ball then heads to the basket for a return pass. Sounds simple, right? Well, it mostly is, but it isn't. After the passer releases the ball, he has several options. For example, he can fake one way, then move in a different direction before he heads to the hoop for a pass and a possible layup. Or he can pretend to be out of the play, then when the defender turns his head or eases up, he darts to the basket to take a pass that can lead to a close-in shot.

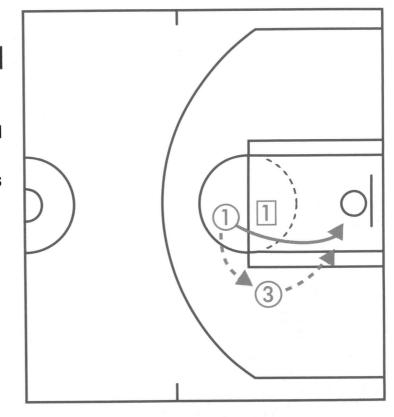

"Not only is the Give-and-Go one of the least complicated plays around, but with the right players involved, it can lead to easy shots. It is especially effective with teammates who have played together for awhile and are familiar with the moves of one another."

LOB PASS

Key players:

Point guard, off guard, small forward, center.

The goal:

To take advantage of a defender who does not get off the ground well. The offensive player should have the hands and the concentration to catch a pass while he is in the air. High flyers Kobe Bryant, Vince Carter, and LeBron James, and big men Dwight Howard and Shaquille O'Neal are known for this very athletic move. If a dunk is the result, the Lob Pass has the potential to change the momentum of the game, as it excites a team and its fans.

How the Lob Pass works:

Usually after a hand or verbal signal, the ball handler lobs a pass over the head of a defender to a teammate near the rim. Ideally, the receiver will catch the ball in mid-air then — look out below! — slam it through the basket before he touches the floor. If the defender is slow to react or the pass is a bit off the line, however, he can catch the ball, come back down, then put it back up for two points.

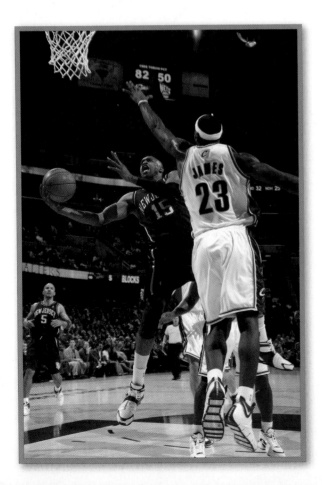

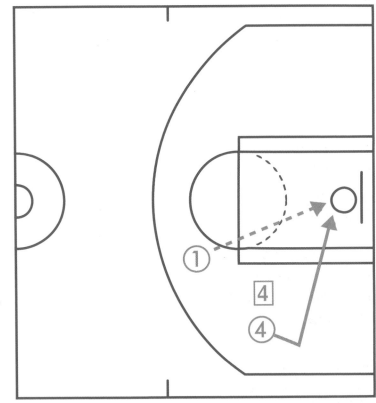

An NBA scout says: "This is the play you see most often on the television highlights every night. Very few athletes can pull it off consistently. When they do, be prepared to pick up your jaw off the floor."

POST-UP

Key players:
Power forward, center.

The goal:
To take advantage of a bigger, stronger, and usually more talented player who is positioned near the basket. In addition to at least one favorite move, the player also should have the ability to pass quickly and accurately, because he is sure to be double-teamed often. Big guys such as Eddy Curry, Tim Duncan, and Shaquille O'Neal have such size and talent that when they get the ball within 10 feet of the basket, it's almost impossible for a single defender to handle them without help from a teammate. (See Double-Team.)

How the Post-Up works:
The offensive player sets up ("posts up") with his back to the basket at either side of the lane. After he receives the ball, the player backs in until he is comfortable enough to attempt a short hook shot or jump shot. The move should be made quick enough so that a second defender cannot come his way. If the defender plays in front of the post player, then the ball can be thrown over his head. (See Lob Pass.)

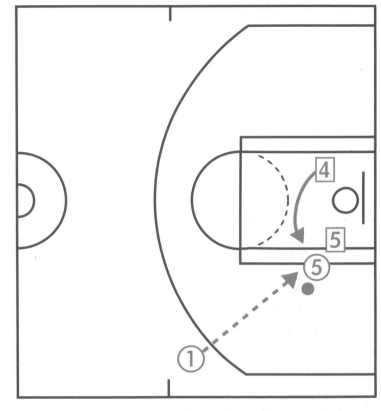

An NBA scout says:
"A big man with post-up skills can make a big difference, but they are not easy to find these days. He can be especially effective in the playoffs, when teams tend to play more cautiously and the pace slows down as a result."

SCREEN AND ROLL

Key players:
Point guard, power forward, center

The goal:
Also known as the "Pick and Roll," this play is intended to confuse the defense, which is forced to think and move quickly on its feet. When done properly, it either slows down the defense, which can result in an open shot for one of two players, or creates a "mismatch" — that is, a smaller defender against a bigger, stronger shooter, or a bigger defender against a smaller, quicker one.

How the Screen And Roll works:
After the ball handler dribbles to a specified area of the court, a teammate moves toward him to screen his defender. (To set a screen, a player plants his feet the width of his shoulders apart. His hands and elbows cannot be used to interfere with the defender, or else he will be whistled for an offensive foul.) After contact is made, the screener moves quickly toward the basket. At that point, the ball handler decides to either pass to the screener if he's open or drive to the basket if he's covered.

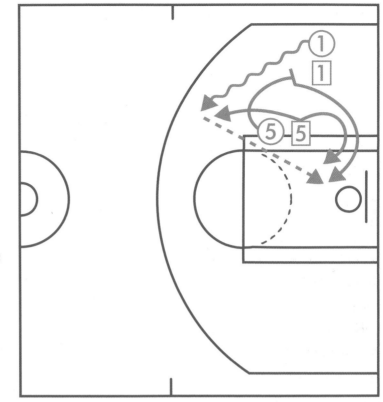

An NBA scout says:
"This is one of the most basic plays in basketball, one that is used in grammar school, high school, college and the pros. Teams with a smart passer and an athletic big man like to call it over and over again until opponents prove they can handle it."

NBA Cares is the league's social responsibility initiative that builds on the NBA's long tradition of addressing important social issues in the United States and around the world. Through this umbrella program, the NBA, its teams, and players have committed to donating $100 million to charity, providing a million hours of hands-on service to the community, and creating 250 places where kids and families can live, learn or play. NBA Cares works with internationally-recognized youth-serving programs that support education, youth and family development, and health-related causes, including: UNICEF; the Make-A-Wish Foundation; and the Global Business Coalition on HIV/AIDS, Malaria and Tuberculosis.

For more information, log on to:

NBA.COM